WITHDRAWN
BY
WILLIAMSBURG REGIONAL LIBRARY

Celebrating YOU and ME

Many Ways to EAT

Williamsburg Regional Library
757-741-3300   www.wrl.org
DEC - - 2022

Christy Peterson

Lerner Publications ◆ Minneapolis

On Sesame Street, we celebrate everyone!

In this series, readers will explore the different ways we eat, dress, play, and more. Recognizing our similarities and differences will teach little ones to be proud of themselves and appreciate the world around them. Together, we can all be smarter, stronger, and kinder.

Sincerely, the Editors at Sesame Workshop

Table of Contents

All Kinds of Foods. 4

Proud to Be Me!. 20

Glossary 22

Learn More. . . 23

Index 24

All Kinds of Foods

Food tells a story about where our families came from. Food can also be a way to learn about other cultures.

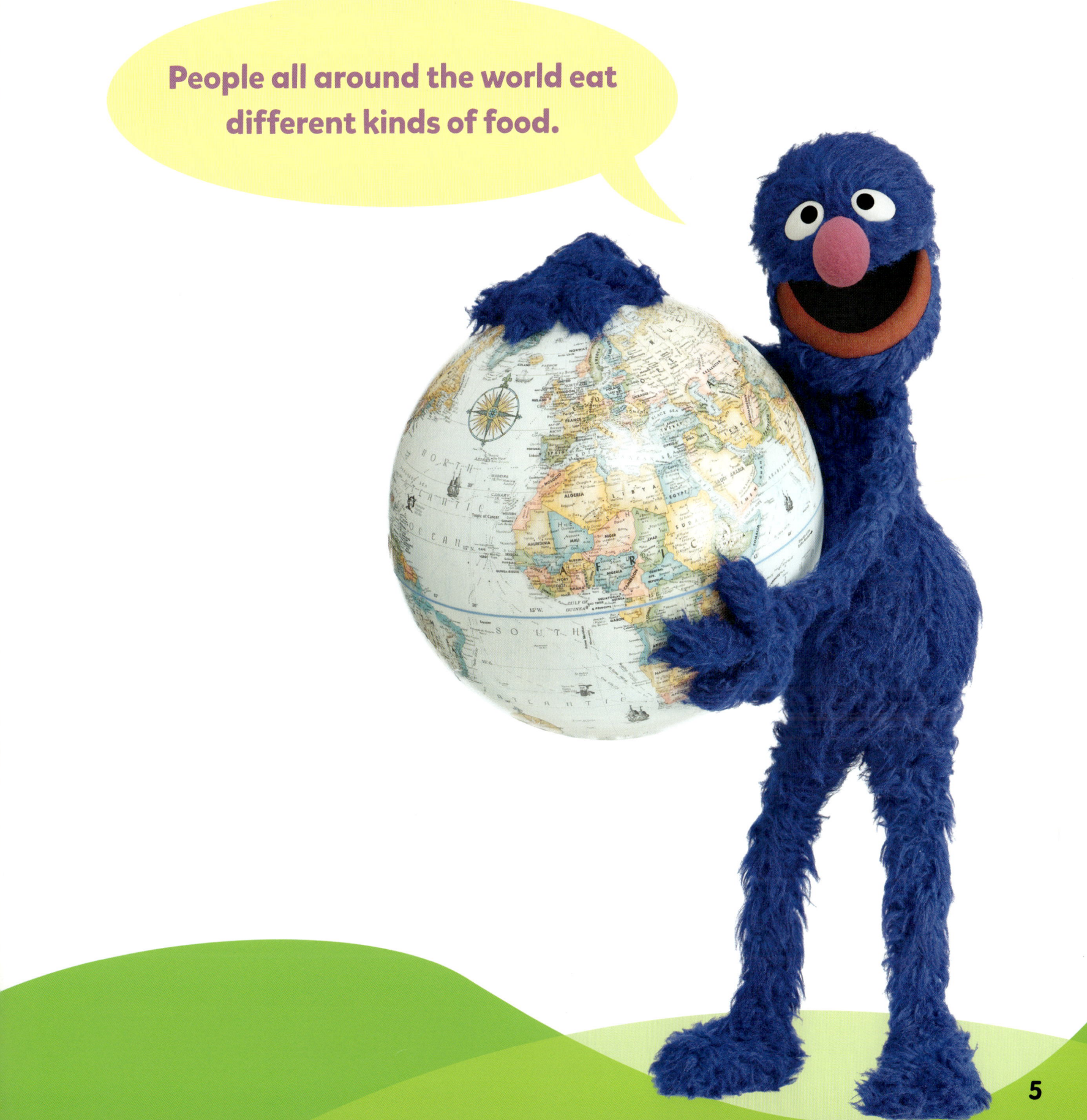

Some foods are specific to a culture.
Other foods are similar around the world.

Foods like rice, bread, and beans are eaten in many countries and cultures. There are many ways to prepare them.

Bread can be all different shapes and sizes.

It can be long, short, flat, or circular.

Some foods, like dumplings, are stuffed with different fillings. For each food, the wrapper and the stuffing are different.

Empanadas are popular in Mexico, samosas are popular in India, and pierogis are popular in Poland.

Places are sometimes known for a kind of food. Many people enjoy rice cakes. In Korea, a type of rice cake called tteokbokki is popular.

Sometimes we eat special food for holidays and celebrations.

On Lunar New Year, people give oranges as gifts for luck. On Jewish New Year, people eat apples dipped in honey for a sweet year.

Jewish New Year is called Rosh Hashanah.

Food brings friends and families from different cultures together.

Proud to Be Me!

What is your favorite food? What are your friends' favorite foods? Draw yourselves sharing your favorite foods with one another.

Glossary

celebration: a gathering held for a special event, like a birthday or a holiday

culture: the beliefs, daily activities, and habits shared by a group of people

holiday: an important cultural or religious event

prepare: to make

tteokbokki: (duk-bo-kee) a kind of rice cake in Korea

Learn More

Bullard, Lisa. *Something Special: All Kinds of Foods*. Minneapolis: Lerner Publications, 2022.

Marie, Lynne. *Let's Eat! Mealtime around the World*. Minneapolis: Beaming Books, 2019.

Reinke, Beth Bence. *Healthy Foods around the World*. Minneapolis: Lerner Publications, 2019.

Index

celebration, 14–16

culture, 4, 6, 8, 18

family, 4, 18

prepare, 8–10

together, 18

Photo Acknowledgments

Image credits: Jose Luis Pelaez Inc/Getty Images, p. 4 (top); Tom Werner/Getty Images, p. 4 (bottom left); Nick Dolding/Getty Images, p. 4 (bottom right); Monkey Business Images/Shutterstock.com, pp. 6, 18 (bottom left); pidjoe/Getty Images, p. 9 (top); apletfx/Getty Images, p. 9 (center left); Creativel/Getty Images, p. 9 (center right); Anthony Boulton/Getty Images, p. 9 (bottom left); AGCuesta/Shutterstock.com, p. 9 (bottom right); zhanghaoran/Shutterstock.com, p. 10; MARCELOKRELLING/Getty Images, p. 11; AS Food studio/Shutterstock.com, p. 12; FangXiaNuo/Getty Images, p. 14; Inna Reznik/Shutterstock.com, p. 17; Ronnachai Palas/Shutterstock.com, p. 18 (top); Jasmin Merdan/Getty Images, p. 18 (bottom right); Inna Kirkorova/Shutterstock.com, p. 20.

Cover: Ned Frisk/Getty Images (top); xavierarnau/Getty Images (center); Jose Luis Pelaez Inc/Getty Images (bottom).

© 2023 Sesame Workshop®, Sesame Street®, and associated characters, trademarks and design elements are owned and licensed by Sesame Workshop. All rights reserved.

International copyright secured. No part of this book may be reproduced, stored in a retrieval system, or transmitted in any form or by any means—electronic, mechanical, photocopying, recording, or otherwise—without the prior written permission of Lerner Publishing Group, Inc., except for the inclusion of brief quotations in an acknowledged review.

Lerner Publications Company
An imprint of Lerner Publishing Group, Inc.
241 First Avenue North
Minneapolis, MN 55401 USA

For reading levels and more information, look up this title at www.lernerbooks.com.

Main body text set in Mikado. Typeface provided by HVD.

Editor: Brianna Kaiser **Designer:** Laura Otto Rinne

Library of Congress Cataloging-in-Publication Data

Names: Peterson, Christy, author.
Title: Many ways to eat / Christy Peterson.
Description: Minneapolis: Lerner Publication , [2023] | Series: Sesame Street Celebrating You and Me | Sesame Street Celebrating Differences: Food. | Includes bibliographical references and index. | Audience: Ages 4–8 years | Audience: Grades K–1 | Summary: "The world offers an amazing variety of delicious foods to try! Join the friendly cast of Sesame Street in learning about foods from many cultures"–Provided by publisher.
Identifiers: LCCN 2021045417 (print) | LCCN 2021045418 (ebook) | ISBN 9781728456195 (Library Binding) | ISBN 9781728463742 (Paperback) | ISBN 9781728462080 (eBook)
Subjects: LCSH: Food habits—Juvenile literature. | Sesame Street (Television program)—Juvenile literature.
Classification: LCC GT2850 .P478 2023 (print) | LCC GT2850 (ebook) | DDC 394.1/2–dc23

LC record available at https://lccn.loc.gov/2021045417
LC ebook record available at https://lccn.loc.gov/2021045418

Manufactured in the United States of America
1-50689-50108-2/2/2022